Living with AI

Navigating the Future Together

Matt Barnette

Chapter 1

Introduction to Artificial Intelligence: Understanding AI in Simple Terms

Exploring the realm of Artificial Intelligence (AI) feels like discovering a hidden stage in your beloved video game, where each twist brings an unexpected delight and every advancement bestows upon you powers beyond belief. AI, our electronic companion, transcends its role from a chess expert to a culinary genius. It's converting the mundane into the remarkable, all happening discreetly in our daily lives.

Imagine a car that knows your destination before you do, weaving through traffic with the finesse of a seasoned taxi driver, all while you kick back and enjoy the ride. This isn't the future; it's what AI is turning into today: a personal chauffeur that doesn't need tips.

But AI doesn't just shine in getting you from point A to point B. It's also moonlighting as a health guru, minus the judgmental glances. Picture an AI in a white coat, sifting through medical data faster than a team of doctors, diagnosing health conditions with the precision of a detective, and tracking your health stats more diligently than a personal trainer ever could. It's like having a mini-hospital at your fingertips, ensuring you stay in tip-top shape without the cold stethoscope feel.

When it comes to entertainment, AI knows how to keep the party going. Whether it's DJing your Friday night with tunes you didn't even know you loved or suggesting movies that perfectly match your mood, AI's got your back. It's like having a personal entertainment guru who always knows how to hit the right note, ensuring your leisure time is never dull.

Shopping with AI takes retail therapy to a new level. Imagine a friend who not only knows your style better than you do but also sniffs out the best deals and remembers every important date and preference. This digital shopping buddy makes sure you're always on point, whether it's finding the perfect birthday gift or snagging that coveted sale item before it's gone.

Yet, with great power comes great responsibility, and AI's ethical conundrum is the plot twist in our story. Navigating the fine line between helpful and invasive, AI stirs up debates worthy of a prime-time drama. The questions it raises about privacy, decision-making, and control are not just theoretical; they're real challenges we face as we integrate AI more deeply into our lives.

In this rapidly evolving world, AI is not just a guest appearance; it's becoming a main character in our daily lives. Its role is complex, filled with potential and pitfalls, making our journey into the future an exciting, sometimes daunting, adventure.

. . .

AI is reshaping our world, making every day a discovery, every task an opportunity to learn and grow. As we navigate this landscape, AI stands by our side, a testament to human ingenuity and a reminder of the mysteries we've yet to unravel.

Welcome to the age of AI, where imagination meets reality, and the future is now. Together, let's embrace the possibilities, face the challenges head-on, and celebrate the marvels of technology that continue to transform our lives in ways we're just beginning to understand.

You know how you sometimes struggle to find the right words? Well, AI is like that friend who always knows what to say. With AI-powered predictive text, composing messages on your phone becomes a breeze. It's like playing a guessing game where AI often wins, finishing your sentences with eerie accuracy. And when it comes to breaking down language barriers, AI transforms into a linguistic superhero, translating foreign languages in real time. It's as if you have a mini United Nations interpreter in your pocket, making sure no language faux pas ruin your day.

Then there's the gaming world, where AI really likes to show off its skills. Imagine playing against an opponent who adapts to your every move, making each game uniquely challenging. That's AI for you, constantly learning and evolving, ensuring you never get bored. But it's not just about making games harder. AI also personalizes your gaming experience, tailoring adventures to suit your style. It's like having a personal game designer on standby, ready to tweak the game environment on the fly to keep you on the edge of your seat.

. . .

Shopping has never been smarter or more convenient, thanks to our AI buddy. Ever wonder how online stores seem to know exactly what you're looking for? That's AI, sifting through mountains of data to find those perfect items, even before you know you want them. It's like having a personal shopper who knows your taste better than you do, ensuring your virtual cart is always filled with goodies you love. And with virtual try-ons, it's as if you have a fitting room right in your living room, minus the awkwardness of undressing in public.

Handling money can be a drag, but AI is here to make even finances feel less daunting. Think of AI as your personal financial advisor, always on hand to offer advice, track your spending, and help you save without the hefty consultation fees. Whether it's setting budget goals or investing in stocks, AI has got your back, making sense of the numbers so you don't have to. It's like turning the complex world of finance into a simple game of Monopoly, where AI helps you navigate the board smartly to avoid going bankrupt.

Education is getting a major boost from AI, transforming learning from a one-size-fits-all approach to a tailored journey that fits each student's pace and style. Imagine an AI tutor that patiently explains math problems or grammar rules until you get it, no eye-rolling or heavy sighs included. It's like having a teacher available 24/7, ready to dive into lessons at a moment's notice, making learning more accessible and engaging for everyone.

As we embrace AI's wonders, it's like opening Pandora's box—filled with ethical questions we can't ignore. The power of AI comes with a responsibility to wield it wisely, ensuring it benefits society without infringing on our privacy or autonomy. It's a delicate dance on the tightrope of innovation, where we must ponder how to let AI enhance our lives without letting it take the wheel completely.

As we've journeyed through the digital landscape, marveling at AI's prowess in simplifying our daily tasks, we've seen it wear many hats: the dutiful assistant, the silent guardian of our homes, and the invisible maestro orchestrating our entertainment. But AI's talents stretch even further, weaving into the fabric of our society in ways we're just beginning to appreciate.

Consider for a moment the humble farm, where the sun rises over fields of crops stretching as far as the eye can see. Here, AI slips on a pair of overalls and becomes the modern farmer's best friend. It's not out there driving the tractor (well, sometimes it is), but it's doing something even more impressive—analyzing soil data, monitoring crop health, and predicting weather patterns to inform planting decisions. It's as if each plant has a personal caretaker, ensuring it grows up strong and healthy. This isn't just farming; it's smart farming, where technology and nature dance in harmony, guided by the gentle hand of AI.

When nature shows its fury, with hurricanes howling and rivers rising, AI steps into the role of the unsung hero. It sifts through satellite images and weather data at lightning speed, predicting disaster paths and helping emergency responders act swiftly. Imagine AI as a vigilant sentinel, perched high above, keeping a watchful eye on impending dangers, ready to sound the alarm. It's the kind of hero that doesn't wear a cape, but its impact is felt by thousands, safeguarding lives and properties by harnessing the power of data and prediction.

. . .

AI's reach extends beyond personal convenience and into the realm of social impact, where it serves as a bridge builder in communities. Through projects that tackle everything from homelessness to providing educational resources in underserved areas, AI is proving to be a valuable ally in the fight for a better world. It analyzes patterns, identifies needs, and helps allocate resources efficiently, embodying the spirit of a social worker with a knack for big data. This is AI wearing its heart on its sleeve, showing us that technology can indeed be a force for good.

As we stand in awe of AI's capabilities, we're also prompted to look in the mirror and ask tough questions about the ethical boundaries of this digital frontier. It's like being at a crossroads, with the power to shape a future where AI serves humanity without compromising our values or freedom. Debates around privacy, data security, and the autonomy of AI-driven decisions are more than just philosophical musings; they're essential dialogues that will define the trajectory of our society. Navigating this landscape requires a balanced approach, blending technological enthusiasm with a steadfast commitment to ethical principles.

From the convenience of our smartphones to the vast fields of smart agriculture, the influence of AI is undeniable. It's a testament to human ingenuity and a reminder of our responsibility to wield such power wisely. As this chapter comes to a close, we're just scratching the surface of AI's potential to transform our world. The adventure into understanding AI in our everyday lives is only beginning, and the path ahead is as exciting as it is uncertain.

. . .

As we turn the page, ready to explore deeper into the realms of AI, we carry with us the lessons of this introductory journey—a mix of wonder, caution, and the unquenchable thirst for knowledge. AI, our quirky digital companion, has much more in store for us, and the future promises to be a tapestry woven with the threads of innovation, challenge, and endless possibility.

Chapter 2

How AI Learns: A Peek into Machine Learning

The world of Artificial Intelligence and machine learning is akin to entering a classroom where computers are the pupils and data serves as the syllabus. Similar to how humans acquire knowledge through experiences, AI assimilates information through exposure to examples. Yet, the question remains: how does this electronic learning mechanism truly function, particularly in tasks like comprehending languages, creating images, or mimicking voices?

Imagine trying to learn a new language not by memorizing vocabulary and grammar rules, but by reading thousands of books in that language, watching movies, and listening to conversations without understanding a single word at first. Sounds daunting, right? Yet, this is similar to how AI learns languages through machine learning models.

. . .

AI uses something called neural networks, which, in a simplified sense, can be thought of as a series of interconnected "neurons" or nodes. These networks don't learn the traditional way humans do; instead, they look for patterns in vast amounts of text data. By analyzing these patterns, AI starts to grasp the structure of the language, the way words form sentences, and how sentences convey meaning.

Now, let's talk about those AI models that can generate images that look like they were taken by a camera or painted by an artist. How does a computer learn to "see" and create? The process is somewhat akin to an artist learning to draw by studying millions of pictures, observing shapes, colors, and textures, and then practicing tirelessly.

Image-generative models are trained on a massive collection of images. Through this training, they learn to recognize and replicate complex patterns, such as the way light falls on an object or how shadows behave. These models don't just copy what they see; they learn the essence of what makes a cat look like a cat or a sunset look like a sunset. When asked to generate an image, the AI uses its learned understanding to create something new, drawing from the patterns and features it has stored during its training.

Voice replication, where AI models can mimic human voices, might seem like something straight out of a sci-fi novel. The secret sauce here is the analysis of audio data. Just as image-generative models study pictures, voice models listen to countless hours of spoken words, learning the nuances of human speech, such as pitch, tone, and rhythm.

. . .

When these models are trained, they analyze the distinctive features of voices, breaking down the sound into understandable components that a computer can manipulate. For voice conversion, the model learns to retain the essence of the spoken words—their meaning and the nuances of language—while altering the audio characteristics to match another voice's pitch, timbre, and speed. It's a complex dance of keeping the content of the message intact while changing its auditory dress.

The magic of AI and machine learning lies in the models' ability to digest enormous amounts of data, learn from patterns, and apply these learnings to create or interpret language, images, and voices in ways that are indistinguishable from human capabilities. It's a testament to the power of data and algorithms, driving home the point that, in the digital age, learning can take on forms beyond our traditional understanding.

The journey AI takes to learn these skills is not just about programming and data; it's about unlocking new potentials in how we communicate, create, and interact with the world around us. As we move forward into the subsequent chapters, we'll dive deeper into specific applications of AI, exploring how this digital learning translates into real-world magic.

When we peel back the curtain on Artificial Intelligence, we find a world of algorithms, data, and processing that transforms raw information into digital knowledge. AI's ability to understand languages, generate images, and replicate human voices hinges on sophisticated training processes involving data preparation, labeling, and the conversion of information into formats AI can understand and learn from.

. . .

Before an AI model can start learning, it needs a dataset to learn from. This dataset is not just a collection of raw data; it's meticulously organized and labeled. Imagine teaching a child to differentiate between cats and dogs. You'd show them pictures of each, clearly saying, "This is a cat" and "This is a dog." In AI training, this process is mirrored through data labeling, where each piece of data (be it an image, text snippet, or audio clip) is tagged with identifying information.

For images, this might mean tagging a photo with labels like "bike," "house," or "tree" to help the AI learn to recognize what these objects look like. The AI model processes thousands, often millions, of these labeled examples during its training phase, learning to associate specific patterns and features with the corresponding labels.

Text data presents a unique challenge: AI models don't understand language as we do. They process information numerically, so text must be converted into a format they can handle. This is where tokenization and encoding come into play. Tokenization breaks down text into manageable pieces, such as words or sentences. Each token is then assigned a unique number, or encoded, transforming the text into a sequence of numbers that the AI model can understand.

Imagine you're assigning a number to every word in the English language. "Cat" might be 123, "jumps" could be 456, and so on. When the AI processes a sentence like "The cat jumps," it sees a sequence of numbers that it learns to associate with certain actions or objects.

. . .

While the concept of binary—representing all data using just zeros and ones—forms the backbone of computing, AI models often deal with more complex representations. Numerical encoding of text, for instance, goes beyond simple binary to include a rich tapestry of values that capture the essence of language in a mathematical form.

AI learns to "see" by processing the numerical values of pixels in images. Each image is essentially a grid of pixels, and each pixel has a numerical value that represents its color intensity. During training, the AI model learns to recognize patterns in these values, identifying shapes, textures, and colors that define various objects.

For image-generative models, training involves not just recognizing these features but also learning how to replicate them. The model learns the distribution of pixel values associated with different objects and uses this knowledge to generate new images that mimic the patterns it has seen during training.

Training voice models involves analyzing the spectral features of audio, such as frequency, pitch, and timbre. Timbre, the quality of sound that lets you distinguish between different voices or instruments even when they're playing the same note, is particularly important. The model learns by dissecting audio samples into these components, understanding the unique signature of each voice.

To replicate or convert voices, AI models analyze these spectral features in training data, learning how to mimic the specific sound qualities of different speakers. When converting one voice to another, the model adjusts these features in the source audio to match the target voice's characteristics, while retaining the original speech content.

The training of AI models is a sophisticated process that involves feeding them vast amounts of labeled data, allowing them to learn from examples. This process is iterative, with the model making predictions based on the data it sees and then adjusting its parameters based on the accuracy of its predictions—a bit like practicing a skill until you get it just right.

For models to learn effectively, they must navigate a vast landscape of data, extracting patterns, and making sense of the information in a way that aligns with their training objectives. This journey from raw data to trained AI model is both complex and fascinating, showcasing the power of algorithms and data in shaping the intelligence of machines.

Understanding how AI models are trained reveals the intricacy and precision involved in turning data into knowledge. From the detailed labeling of datasets to the numerical transformation of text and the spectral analysis of audio, each step in the training process is a testament to the incredible capabilities of modern AI. As we delve deeper into the applications and implications of these technologies in the following chapters, we'll continue to explore the remarkable ways in which AI models learn, adapt, and transform the world around us.

Chapter 3

The Brain of AI: Exploring Neural Networks

In the bustling corridors of our metaphorical high school, every whisper and rumor contributes to the ever-evolving story, mimicking how neural networks refine their understanding through each layer of processing. The dynamics of this gossip network beautifully parallel the workings of neural networks, where each student (or neuron) plays a part in shaping the final outcome, based on the snippets of information they receive and pass on.

Imagine a neural network tasked with understanding human speech or recognizing faces in photos. It doesn't start out knowing how to perform these tasks. Instead, it learns through exposure—much like our high school network learns the nuances of gossip. The network is fed examples, each one processed through multiple layers, where it learns to identify patterns: the intonation in a voice that indicates a question or the particular arrangement of features that defines a face.

. . .

This learning process isn't so different from how rumors spread and evolve. With each retelling, the story might gain a new detail or lose an old one, altering slightly to fit the context of the conversation or the biases of the speaker. Similarly, as data moves through a neural network, it's transformed, adjusted by weights and biases—the network's mathematical equivalents of personal interpretation.

However, there's a key difference in how this information is handled. In the high school gossip network, accuracy might not be the top priority; excitement and intrigue often win out. Neural networks, on the other hand, strive for precision. Their configurations are constantly tweaked based on feedback, a process known as training. When a network makes a prediction, that prediction is compared against the truth, and adjustments are made. This is akin to someone correcting a rumor with the real story, refining the network's ability to discern truth from fiction.

As neural networks train, they become increasingly sophisticated, learning to ignore irrelevant details and focus on what truly matters for the task at hand. This might mean learning to filter out background noise in a voice command or distinguishing a cat from a dog in a photo, regardless of the photo's quality or the animal's pose.

The beauty of this system lies in its flexibility and depth. Just as a rumor can spread through different cliques, gaining complexity and nuance, neural networks can handle increasingly complex tasks, from driving cars autonomously to translating languages in real-time. They do this by building on simple concepts, layer by layer, to form a detailed understanding of the world.

. . .

As we close this chapter on neural networks, it's clear that the comparison to high school gossip does more than offer a chuckle. It illuminates the complexity of AI learning in an approachable way, highlighting how information—whether it's a piece of gossip or a data point—transforms and evolves as it moves through networks, shaping the intelligence of the systems that rely on it.

Understanding neural networks is a key step in demystifying AI, revealing the mechanisms that enable machines to learn from data, make decisions, and, in some ways, think. As we move forward, we'll continue to explore the myriad ways in which AI and machine learning impact our lives, always aiming to unravel the complexity of these technologies with humor, clarity, and sharp observations.

In the grand scheme of things, our high school gossip network does more than just pass information around; it serves as a living, breathing system that learns, evolves, and occasionally, stumbles upon the truth amidst a sea of rumors. This dynamic is remarkably similar to how neural networks operate, constantly refining their understanding and improving their predictions through layers of input and feedback.

Consider the way a rumor starts, perhaps with something as simple as "Did you see Alex's new skateboard?" By the time this question has made its rounds, it might transform into "Alex is a skateboarding pro now!" This transformation—though it might add a dash of exaggeration—carries the core truth: Alex has a new skateboard. Neural networks function under a similar principle, taking input data (Alex has a new skateboard), processing it through various layers (exaggerations and interpretations), and outputting a refined understanding or prediction (Alex is into skateboarding).

. . .

This process of transformation and refinement is not random; it's guided by the structure and configuration of the network. Each layer within a neural network specializes in identifying and processing different aspects of the data it receives. The first layer might recognize basic patterns or features, while deeper layers combine these initial findings into more complex interpretations. This hierarchical processing mirrors how gossip can evolve from simple observations to complex narratives as it travels through the student body.

Training a neural network is akin to schooling our gossip network in discerning fact from fiction. Through exposure to countless examples and continuous feedback, neural networks learn to filter out noise and focus on relevant patterns. This learning process is meticulous and requires a vast amount of data, ensuring that the network can handle a wide range of scenarios with accuracy and reliability.

As neural networks evolve, they become capable of tackling tasks of increasing complexity, from distinguishing cats and dogs in photos to navigating the intricacies of human language in natural language processing systems. The key to their success lies in their ability to learn from examples, adapting their internal parameters (weights and biases) to improve performance over time. This adaptability is what makes neural networks so powerful, enabling them to master tasks that require understanding subtle patterns and nuances.

Yet, for all their sophistication, neural networks, much like our high school gossipers, are not infallible. They can be misled by biased data, overfit to specific examples, or fail to generalize their learning to new, unseen situations. The challenges of training neural networks—

ensuring they are accurate, unbiased, and capable of generalization—reflect the ongoing efforts within the field of AI to create systems that are not only intelligent but also fair and reliable.

As we wrap up our exploration of neural networks through the lens of high school gossip, it's clear that this metaphor offers more than just a playful comparison. It sheds light on the complex processes that underpin AI learning, highlighting both the capabilities and challenges of neural networks in a way that's accessible and engaging. As we continue our journey through the world of Artificial Intelligence, we carry with us a deeper understanding of how these technologies learn, grow, and, occasionally, surprise us with their insights and abilities.

In the chapters to come, we'll delve into further applications of AI, exploring how these principles of learning and adaptation are applied across various domains, from healthcare and finance to entertainment and beyond. With each step, we aim to demystify the workings of AI, making the incredible science behind these technologies as relatable and understandable as the stories shared within the walls of a high school.

Chapter 4

AI in Your Pocket: Smartphones and Gadgets

Imagine your smartphone is not just a phone but a ninja personal assistant, always lurking in the shadows, ready to jump out with a helpful tip, a reminder, or even to take over tasks you'd rather avoid. This ninja doesn't wear a black suit or carry a sword; its tools are algorithms, data, and a seamless interface with the world around you. This is the role of AI in your pocket—silent, efficient, and always on guard.

Every time you ask your phone a question, whether it's about the weather tomorrow or who won the World Series in 1986, AI is at work, sifting through the internet's vast knowledge to bring you the answer. But its talents don't stop at being your personal quiz champion. This digital ninja makes sure your photos are picture-perfect, your emails are spam-free, and your schedule runs like a well-oiled machine, all without you noticing its presence.

. . .

Think about the last time you took a photo with your phone. Did you notice how it suggested the best frame or automatically enhanced the lighting? That's AI, quietly analyzing millions of pixels in milliseconds, ensuring that your snapshot looks like it was taken by a pro photographer. It learns from countless images to recognize faces, smiles, and even your pet's quirky expressions, adjusting settings in the blink of an eye to capture every moment in its best light.

Now, let's dive into how your phone seems to know you better than you know yourself. It predicts the words you're about to type, saving you precious seconds and often, the embarrassment of typos. It learns from your typing habits, favorite phrases, and even your most used emojis, tailoring its predictions to fit your style. This personalized experience is courtesy of AI's ability to learn and adapt, creating a unique interaction that feels almost human.

But AI's role extends beyond convenience; it's also your first line of defense against digital threats. With cyber-attacks becoming more sophisticated, your ninja assistant stays vigilant, scanning apps for malicious behavior and filtering out phishing attempts disguised as harmless emails. It's constantly learning from new threats, ensuring that your digital life is secure, safeguarding your personal information from unseen dangers.

As we interact with our gadgets, AI is always working in the background, orchestrating our digital experience with precision and care. It manages battery life, ensuring your phone lasts through the day by predicting which apps you're likely to use and which can be put to sleep. It connects you with the world, optimizing network settings for a seamless internet experience, whether you're streaming your favorite show or video-calling a friend on the other side of the globe.

In the realm of wearables, AI transforms ordinary gadgets into personal health coaches. It tracks your steps, monitors your heart rate, and even nudges you to stand up and move around if you've been sitting for too long. By analyzing your activity patterns, it offers personalized fitness advice, encouraging you to reach your health goals in a way that feels supportive and non-intrusive.

As we continue to explore AI's invisible yet indispensable role in our smartphones and gadgets, it becomes clear that this technology is not just about making life easier or more entertaining. It's about enhancing our human experience, providing us with tools and insights that help us live better, healthier, and more connected lives. This digital ninja, always in the background, always ready to assist, is a testament to the incredible potential of AI to transform the mundane into the extraordinary.

In the next part of this chapter, we'll delve even deeper into the ways AI integrates into our daily routines, exploring its impact on everything from navigation to online shopping, and how it continues to learn and evolve alongside us, always anticipating our needs and exceeding our expectations.

Venturing beyond the immediate convenience and security AI provides, let's consider its role in the realm of navigation and travel. Have you ever marveled at how your smartphone can predict traffic conditions, suggesting the fastest route to your destination? This predictive power is AI at work, analyzing real-time data from countless sources to guide you through the maze of city streets with ease. It's like having a local guide in your pocket, one who knows every shortcut and traffic jam, ensuring you're always on the best path.

But AI's influence doesn't stop at getting you from point A to point B; it extends into the very fabric of our daily routines, including how we shop and make decisions. Online shopping, for instance, has been revolutionized by AI's ability to understand our preferences and habits. It curates personalized recommendations, almost as if it's reading our minds, showing us products we're likely to want before we even realize it ourselves. This personal shopper aspect of AI saves us time and introduces us to new products that fit our tastes, making the shopping experience both efficient and enjoyable.

Furthermore, AI in gadgets has made the leap into home automation, turning ordinary homes into smart environments. Lights adjust to our preferences, thermostats learn our schedules to ensure comfort while optimizing energy use, and smart speakers play our favorite music with just a voice command. This level of personalization and automation is akin to having a butler who anticipates your needs, always one step ahead in making your home more welcoming and efficient.

One of the most personal touches AI brings into our lives is through health and wellness monitoring. Through wearable devices, AI keeps an eye on our physical well-being, tracking activities, sleep patterns, and even nutrition. It's not just about counting steps or monitoring heart rates; AI uses this data to provide insights and recommendations tailored to our health goals. It's like a personal coach who's always there, encouraging and guiding us towards healthier choices, all based on data that's unique to us.

As AI continues to evolve, it's pushing the boundaries of what's possible with gadgets. We're seeing the emergence of AI-powered translation devices that allow for real-time conversation with people who speak different languages, breaking down barriers and opening up new possibilities for connection and understanding. This technology, once the stuff of science fiction, is now a reality, enabling us to explore and interact with the world in ways we never thought possible.

In crafting these experiences, AI doesn't just follow instructions blindly. It learns, adapts, and even predicts, constantly refining its algorithms to better serve our needs. This ongoing learning process is what makes AI so powerful and so integral to the future of technology. It's not just about the tasks AI can perform today; it's about the potential for even more personalized, intuitive, and helpful interactions in the future.

As we wrap up our exploration of AI in smartphones and gadgets, it's clear that this technology is not just an add-on or a feature; it's a fundamental part of how we interact with the digital world. AI has become the ultimate backstage crew member, invisible yet indispensable, enhancing every aspect of our digital lives. From the moment we wake up to the moment we go to sleep, AI is there, making our lives easier, safer, and more connected.

Looking ahead, the possibilities are as limitless as our imagination. As AI technology advances, we can expect even more innovative and transformative applications to emerge, further integrating digital intelligence into our daily lives. The journey with AI is just beginning, and the future promises to be as exciting as it is unpredictable.

Chapter 5

Your Home, Smart and Automated

In the world of tomorrow that we're lucky enough to live in today, our homes have gotten a serious upgrade, evolving from mere brick and mortar to intelligent entities that seem to think and breathe on their own. This transformation is all thanks to Artificial Intelligence, the silent powerhouse turning our living spaces into realms of convenience, comfort, and downright coolness.

Picture this: an invisible butler, tirelessly working round the clock, managing everything from the temperature to the tunes that greet you when you walk in. But this isn't your typical butler from the stories of olden days; no, this butler is a modern marvel, a network of smart devices and AI algorithms that ensure your home runs smoother than a well-oiled machine.

Now, imagine an ant colony—yes, you read that right, ants. These tiny creatures are nature's experts at organization and efficiency, with every ant knowing its job without being handed a to-do list every morning. In our smart homes, AI operates with the same level of precision and purpose. Lights know when to dim as the sun sets, thermostats adjust the temperature for optimal comfort with no need for human intervention, and security systems keep vigilant watch over our safety, all orchestrated by the unseen hand of AI.

The magic of a smart home lies in its ability to learn and adapt. Just like you'd get to know a human butler over time, your AI butler gets to know you—your preferences, routines, and even those quirky habits you thought nobody noticed. It learns that you like the living room cozy and the lights bright when you're reading, but prefer the ambiance soft and the music low when hosting dinner parties.

This learning isn't just about making life easier (though, let's be honest, that's a pretty big perk); it's about creating a home that truly feels like an extension of yourself. Your smart home, powered by AI, doesn't just respond to your commands; it anticipates your needs, adjusting the environment to suit your mood or the task at hand, all without you having to lift a finger.

And let's not forget about the energy-saving superhero aspect of your AI butler. By optimizing the use of appliances and systems, it ensures that you're not only comfortable but also eco-friendly, reducing waste and saving on bills. It's like having a personal environmentalist assessing every watt and drop of water, making sure your castle is as green as it is grand.

But what about those times when things don't go as planned? Like when you're running late and forget to turn off the lights or adjust the thermostat. Fear not, for your AI butler has got your back, managing these tasks with the finesse of a chess master making their winning move. It keeps your home safe, secure, and running efficiently, even when you're miles away, providing peace of mind that's priceless in today's fast-paced world.

As we dig in to the workings of smart homes, it becomes clear that AI is not just a tool or a fancy gadget; it's the heartbeat of a home that knows and understands its inhabitants. This seamless integration of technology into our domestic lives is transforming the very concept of what it means to be "at home," turning our living spaces into responsive environments that cater to our needs, desires, and whims in ways we've only dreamed of.

Navigating through the ecosystem of a smart home, we encounter more than just automated lights and thermostats; we step into a world where every gadget and appliance speaks a language of efficiency and personalization, orchestrated by the silent conductor that is AI. This isn't about technology taking over; it's about technology lending a hand, making life not just easier but also more enjoyable.

Consider the morning routine: your alarm gently wakes you up, not with a jarring ring, but with your favorite upbeat song. The curtains draw themselves back, revealing the soft morning light, while your coffee maker brews a perfect cup just the way you like it. And all this happens without you uttering a single word. It's like your home knows exactly how to start your day on the right foot—thanks to the AI butler who's been paying attention.

This level of personalization extends to entertainment. Your smart TV doesn't just offer a myriad of channels; it suggests shows and movies based on what you love, transforming the endless scroll into a curated selection that hits the mark every time. It's like having a friend who knows your taste in movies and always has the best recommendations up their sleeve.

But the intelligence of a smart home isn't limited to managing routines and preferences; it also plays a critical role in health and well-being. Imagine air purifiers that adjust their settings based on the quality of indoor air, ensuring you breathe clean air, or smart mirrors that offer health and fitness advice. These aren't futuristic fantasies; they're real-life applications of AI working tirelessly to enhance our physical and mental health, proving that smart homes care as much about our well-being as we do.

Moreover, the AI butler in our smart homes is a master of resource management. It meticulously monitors water and energy consumption, identifying opportunities to reduce waste. Leaky faucet? Your AI butler alerts you before it becomes a problem. Lights left on in an empty room? They're turned off automatically. It's as if your home is on a mission to be as eco-friendly as possible, championing sustainability without compromising on comfort.

Yet, for all its capabilities, the true brilliance of AI in smart homes lies in its subtlety. It doesn't boast about its achievements or demand recognition. Instead, it works quietly behind the scenes, ensuring your home is a place where you can relax, recharge, and connect with loved ones in a space that feels uniquely yours.

As we conclude our journey through the smart, automated home, it's clear that AI is more than just an invisible butler; it's a guardian, a personal assistant, and a friend rolled into one. It represents a new era of living where technology and personal space merge to create environments that are not only smart but also intuitive, responsive, and deeply connected to our needs and preferences.

The future of smart homes is bright, with endless possibilities for innovation and improvement. As AI technology evolves, so too will the capabilities of our homes, offering us glimpses into a world where our living spaces are not just where we reside but are partners in our quest for a better, more fulfilling life.

Chapter 6

AI on the Move: Transportation and Navigation

Welcome to the high-speed, ever-shifting world of transportation, where Artificial Intelligence has taken the driver's seat, steering us into a future that feels straight out of a sci-fi movie. But don't worry, this isn't a tale of robots taking over; it's the story of how AI, our savvy local guide, is making getting from point A to point B not just easier, but a journey worth savoring.

Imagine you're in a bustling city, trying to find the best coffee shop that only the locals know about. In the world powered by AI, your smartphone becomes your best friend, whispering the secrets of the city into your ear. It navigates you through winding streets, past the crowded main roads, and straight to that hidden gem of a café, all while avoiding traffic jams like a pro. This isn't just smart navigation; it's AI knowing the pulse of the city better than a heartbeat.

. . .

But AI's role in transportation goes beyond playing tour guide. It's transforming the very essence of how we move. Take self-driving cars, for example. These aren't just vehicles; they're brainy companions on wheels, equipped with eyes (sensors) and brains (AI algorithms) that see and think. They can predict the unpredictable, like a cyclist suddenly darting across the road, and make split-second decisions that keep everyone safe. It's like having a superhero chauffeur at your beck and call, only instead of a cape, it wears a sleek coat of paint.

And it's not just cars that AI is revolutionizing. Public transport is getting a smart makeover too. Buses and trains that know exactly when to arrive and depart, minimizing wait times and making our commutes smoother than a buttered slide. These aren't fantasies; they're the present-day miracles of AI, working tirelessly behind the scenes to orchestrate the symphony of city life.

Now, let's zoom out a bit and look at the bigger picture—air travel. Here, AI steps in as the master planner, managing flight schedules, optimizing routes, and ensuring safety in the skies. It's like having a guardian angel for every plane, guiding them through the vast blue, ensuring every journey is as safe as it is efficient.

But what truly sets AI apart in the world of transportation isn't just its ability to guide, drive, or manage. It's its relentless pursuit of improvement. AI learns from every journey, every hiccup in traffic, and every twist in the road. It's constantly evolving, finding new ways to make our travels faster, safer, and more enjoyable. It's not just about getting to your destination; it's about making the journey worthwhile.

. . .

In the first half of this chapter, we've seen how AI, our digital local guide, is reshaping the landscape of transportation and navigation. From whispering city secrets to driving us home safely, AI is the unseen force propelling us into a future where every journey is tailored just for us, making the world a little smaller, a little closer, and a lot more connected.

Stay tuned for the next part, where we'll dive even deeper into the marvels of AI in transportation, exploring how this technology continues to push the boundaries of what's possible on the road, in the skies, and beyond.

As we continue our high-speed journey through the realms of transportation revolutionized by AI, let's explore further how this technology is not just reshaping our travel experiences but also redefining efficiency and safety on a grand scale.

Beyond the roads and the individual adventures, AI plays a critical role in logistics and freight, acting as the brain behind the seamless movement of goods around the globe. Imagine a world where your online shopping orders arrive faster than ever before, not because of magic, but thanks to AI-driven logistics that optimize routes, manage inventories, and predict delivery times with astonishing accuracy. It's like having a personal shopper who not only knows exactly what you want but also the quickest way to get it to your doorstep.

But how does AI manage to keep this complex dance of transportation so elegantly synchronized? It's all about data—the lifeblood of AI. By analyzing patterns from vast amounts of information, AI predicts traffic conditions, weather disruptions, and even potential system breakdowns before they happen. It's akin to having a crystal ball, but instead of mystical powers, it uses algorithms and machine learning to foresee the future of transportation logistics, ensuring that the global supply chain moves like a well-choreographed ballet.

Let's not forget the environmental aspect. AI isn't just about speed and convenience; it's also about making transportation greener. Electric vehicles (EVs) and AI form a dynamic duo fighting against pollution. AI optimizes battery usage and driving patterns, extending the range of EVs and making them a more viable option for more people. It's like having an eco-warrior riding shotgun, helping you make choices that are kinder to the planet.

In the public sphere, AI is revolutionizing how we view public transportation. Imagine city buses and trains that run with such precision that you never have to run for a bus again, only to watch it pull away as you reach the stop. AI in public transport systems analyzes passenger data, adjusts routes and schedules in real-time, and even predicts future needs to accommodate growing urban populations. This isn't just convenience; it's about creating sustainable, accessible cities where public transport is a reliable, enjoyable option for everyone.

And for those who dream of taking to the skies without the hassle of traditional air travel, AI is working on something for you too. Urban air mobility, powered by AI, promises a future where small, automated aircraft could whisk us across cityscapes, soaring over traffic jams and crowded streets. It's like having a personal magic carpet, powered by the most advanced AI, ready to take urban transportation to new heights.

. . .

As we navigate through the ever-evolving landscape of AI in transportation and navigation, it's clear that we're not just passengers on this journey; we're co-pilots, alongside AI, exploring the frontiers of what's possible. From making our daily commutes smoother and safer to transforming the global supply chain and reducing our carbon footprint, AI is the driving force behind a transportation revolution that's just getting started.

In wrapping up this chapter on AI's role in transportation, we've seen how AI acts as a local guide, a logistics mastermind, an environmental advocate, and a visionary for future urban mobility. The road ahead is exciting, filled with opportunities for innovation, improvement, and, most importantly, for making our world more connected and sustainable. With AI in the driver's seat, we're on the fast track to a future where transportation is not just about getting from point A to point B; it's about the journey, the experience, and the positive impact we can make along the way.

Chapter 7

Healthcare and AI: A Partnership for the Future

In the realm of epidemiology, AI acts like a global detective, sifting through digital clues to track disease patterns and outbreaks. This isn't about eavesdropping on personal conversations but analyzing vast amounts of public data to identify trends that could indicate the spread of infections. By parsing through news articles, social media posts, and healthcare reports, AI can alert health authorities about potential outbreaks before they spiral out of control. It's as if we have a guardian constantly scanning the horizon for threats, ready to sound the alarm at the first sign of trouble, ensuring that preparation and prevention measures are set in motion swiftly.

Turning our attention to telehealth, AI has revolutionized the way we access medical care, especially in times when visiting a doctor in person isn't feasible. Through virtual consultations, AI serves as the backbone, ensuring that doctors have all the necessary information at their fingertips. It can analyze a patient's medical history, compare symptoms against vast databases of medical knowledge, and even suggest potential diagnoses. This system doesn't replace doctors but enhances their ability to make informed decisions, akin to a detective piecing together clues to solve a case, with AI shining a flashlight on the most critical evidence.

Furthermore, AI has made significant strides in personalizing patient care. Through machine learning algorithms, healthcare providers can offer treatments tailored to the individual's genetic makeup, lifestyle, and health history. This precision medicine approach ensures that treatments are not only more effective but also come with fewer side effects. Imagine your healthcare plan as a custom-made suit, designed to fit you perfectly, rather than a one-size-fits-all garment that never quite matches your needs.

AI's superhero status in healthcare is also evident in its role in mental health support. With the increasing prevalence of mental health issues, AI-powered apps provide a listening ear, offering coping strategies and monitoring users' mental well-being. These apps can't replace human therapists, but they can offer support and guidance, making mental health resources more accessible to those who might not otherwise seek help.

As we conclude our journey through the landscape of AI in healthcare, it's clear that AI's role is both vast and nuanced. From acting as a global watchdog for disease outbreaks to personalizing patient care and supporting mental health, AI's contributions are indispensable. It operates behind the scenes, tirelessly working to make healthcare more accessible, effective, and personalized. In this era of technological advancement, AI stands as a silent guardian, a beacon of hope, and a promise of a healthier future for all.

· · ·

This exploration of AI in healthcare illustrates the technology's diverse applications, underscoring its potential to transform patient care, disease prevention, and the overall healthcare landscape. If there are additional aspects you're curious about or specific directions you'd like the narrative to take, please let me know how I can further assist.

As AI becomes an increasingly integral part of the healthcare landscape, navigating the ethical landscape is paramount. Ensuring that AI-driven solutions are developed and used with a keen sense of responsibility is akin to a superhero adhering to a moral code. The data that fuels AI's insights in healthcare is deeply personal, making privacy and security top priorities. Striking the right balance between leveraging AI for groundbreaking advancements and protecting individual rights is the ongoing challenge for the guardians of this technology.

Inclusivity and access also stand out as critical areas where AI must prove its worth as a force for good in healthcare. The potential to democratize access to high-quality healthcare services, making them available to underserved populations around the globe, is one of AI's most compelling promises. Achieving this requires a concerted effort to design AI tools that are as universally accessible as they are advanced, ensuring that the benefits of AI in healthcare reach far and wide, transcending geographical and socioeconomic barriers.

Looking ahead, the role of AI in healthcare is poised for exponential growth. Innovations on the horizon promise to further blur the lines between science fiction and medical reality. Imagine AI systems capable of providing real-time guidance to surgeons during complex procedures or virtual health assistants accessible from the comfort of one's home, offering expert advice around the clock. The future holds the promise of AI not only responding to health queries but also anticipating health needs before they become apparent, offering a proactive approach to wellness and disease prevention.

This future, however, hinges on the collective effort of technologists, healthcare professionals, ethicists, and policymakers to guide the development and application of AI in healthcare. It requires a shared vision that places human well-being at the center of technological innovation, ensuring that AI serves as a tool for enhancing, not replacing, the human touch in healthcare.

As this chapter on AI in healthcare concludes, it's clear that AI's role is akin to that of a superhero sidekick—powerful, dedicated, and driven by a mission to serve and protect. Yet, the true power of AI in healthcare lies in its potential to empower individuals and healthcare providers alike, offering tools and insights that make healthier lives possible. The journey of AI in healthcare is just beginning, and its path is lined with both challenges and opportunities. Embracing this journey with caution, creativity, and compassion can turn the promise of AI into a reality that benefits all of humanity.

Chapter 8

AI in Entertainment and Creativity

In the bustling world of entertainment, where the spotlight often shines on the stars we see and the voices we hear, there lurks an unsung hero in the shadows. This hero doesn't seek applause or bask in the glow of the limelight. Instead, it works tirelessly, weaving the magic that transforms entertainment into a personalized journey for each of us. This maestro, the genius behind the curtain, is none other than Artificial Intelligence.

Imagine walking into a room that knows your mood just by the look on your face and plays the perfect song to lift your spirits. It's not magic; it's AI, the DJ who knows your music library better than you do. With a few swipes on your smartphone, AI sifts through your playlists, analyzing beats, lyrics, and rhythms, crafting a soundtrack that feels like it was made just for you.

But AI's talents extend far beyond playing DJ at your impromptu dance parties. It's also the creative genius behind your favorite movies and video games, working in the background to ensure the stories unfold in ways that captivate your imagination. In video games, AI is the puppet master, controlling characters that adapt to your play style, making every battle more challenging and every adventure unique. It learns from your every move, ensuring that no two game-plays are ever the same, making you the hero in a story that's constantly evolving.

Now, let's talk about movies and how AI is transforming them into interactive experiences. Imagine choosing the path the storyline takes, with characters responding to your decisions, leading to different endings. AI scripts these dynamic narratives, allowing you to step into the director's chair and shape the story as it unfolds. This isn't just watching a movie; it's living it.

In the realm of creativity, AI plays the role of both muse and artisan. Artists and musicians are collaborating with AI to push the boundaries of their crafts. AI algorithms analyze styles and techniques, suggesting new lines of melody or strokes of the brush that complement the creator's vision. It's like having a creative sidekick that never runs out of ideas, inspiring artists to explore uncharted territories in their work.

But perhaps the most spellbinding trick up AI's sleeve is its ability to generate art and music on its own. Given a theme or emotion to express, AI can create paintings, compose music, or write stories that resonate with human emotions. This isn't about replacing human creativity but augmenting it, opening doors to new forms of expression that were previously unimaginable.

· · ·

As we've journeyed through the world of entertainment and creativity, it's clear that AI, our behind-the-scenes maestro, plays a pivotal role in shaping experiences that are deeply personal and endlessly innovative. It doesn't just understand our preferences; it anticipates them, crafting moments of joy, wonder, and inspiration that feel tailor-made for us.

This exploration into AI's involvement in entertainment and creativity only scratches the surface of its potential. As technology advances, the partnership between AI and human creativity promises to bring forth experiences that are more immersive, interactive, and personalized, transforming the way we see, hear, and feel the world of entertainment.

As we delve deeper into the role of AI in entertainment and creativity, it becomes evident that this digital maestro is not just working behind the scenes; it's revolutionizing the very fabric of how we interact with the arts, making every experience more engaging and uniquely ours.

In the world of literature, AI has begun to weave its narratives, crafting stories that adapt to the reader's preferences. Imagine a book that changes its plot based on your reactions, leading you down different paths with every choice you make. It's like being in a choose-your-own-adventure story, but where the possibilities are endless, and the outcomes are crafted by an intelligence that learns from your every decision.

But what about creating art? AI doesn't just suggest; it generates. Using deep learning, it can produce artworks in the style of famous painters, or entirely new pieces that defy traditional classification. It's as if there's a virtual Picasso in your computer, ready to collaborate on a masterpiece or inspire you to create your own. This isn't about replacing human artists but offering a new brush, a different palette for creators to experiment with, expanding the horizons of what's possible in art.

Let's not forget the magic AI brings to the movie industry. Beyond suggesting which movie you might enjoy on a Friday night, AI analyzes scripts to predict box office success, helping studios decide which projects to greenlight. It's the ultimate critic, but one that's more interested in numbers and patterns than in plot and character development. Yet, in doing so, AI ensures that the movies reaching our screens have that special something that resonates with audiences, making our movie-watching experiences all the more thrilling.

AI's involvement doesn't stop at creation and curation; it also extends to the way we experience entertainment. Virtual reality (VR) and augmented reality (AR), powered by AI, are changing the game, creating immersive worlds that feel as real as our own. In these virtual spaces, you're not just a spectator; you're part of the story, interacting with characters and environments in ways that were once the domain of imagination alone. It's as if AI has handed us the keys to a kingdom where the only limit is our creativity.

As we wrap up our exploration of AI's role in entertainment and creativity, it's clear that this technological maestro is playing a symphony of innovation. From personalized music playlists to interactive storytelling, and from digital art to immersive cinematic experiences, AI is not just changing the way we consume entertainment; it's transforming how we perceive creativity itself. It invites us to be not just consumers but creators, participants in a world where technology and imagination dance together in harmony.

43

The future of entertainment, shaped by AI, promises to be one where personalized experiences are the norm, where creativity knows no bounds, and where every one of us can find our tune, our story, our masterpiece. It's a world where the line between creator and audience blurs, giving rise to new forms of expression and engagement. In this ever-evolving landscape, AI stands as a testament to human ingenuity, a reminder that our capacity to dream and create is amplified, not diminished, by the machines we build.

As we look forward to this dazzling future, one thing is certain: the role of AI in entertainment and creativity is only just beginning to unfold. Its full potential is yet to be discovered, but one thing is clear —AI, the unsung hero of the digital age, is set to take us on an unforgettable journey, redefining the very essence of what it means to be entertained and inspired.

Chapter 9

Shopping and AI: Tailoring the Retail Experience

Going on a shopping adventure in the era of technology is akin to having a companion who understands you more intimately than you understand yourself, and this companion isn't a person—it's Artificial Intelligence, acting as your individual shopping guide. Imagine this scenario: you're navigating the virtual shelves of your preferred online marketplace when, out of nowhere, you receive suggestions so accurate, it feels as though they've peeked into your thoughts. This isn't happenstance; it's the result of AI casting its spell, customizing your shopping journey to match your likes, dislikes, and even those annoying allergies you'd rather not deal with.

Imagine walking into a store where the clerk knows your name, your style preferences, the food you love, and the brands you loathe. Now, transplant that idea into the digital realm, and you've got AI—a know-it-all shopping pal that tracks your online browsing with the precision of a detective. It remembers that you lingered on a page with sci-fi novels but breezed past the romance section. It notes your penchant for peanut butter but logs your allergy to nuts. It's a bit like having a stalker, but instead of creepy, it's incredibly helpful.

Clothes shopping online can feel like a gamble. Will it fit? Will it look good? Here comes AI, donning its superhero cape, ready to save the day. Through sophisticated algorithms that analyze your past purchases and returns, AI predicts what size you need in different brands. It's like having a tailor who's never met you but somehow knows exactly how to make clothes fit you perfectly. And with virtual fitting rooms, it's as if you're trying on outfits in the future, where mirrors give you a 360-degree preview without ever having to leave your room.

AI doesn't just help with finding the right products; it's also your ally in snagging the best deals. Picture a bloodhound, tirelessly sniffing out bargains across the internet. That's AI, tirelessly scouring through databases for price drops, coupon codes, and flash sales, ensuring you never overpay. It's like having a personal bargain hunter at your fingertips, one that doesn't require coffee breaks or gets tired.

Ever struggled with finding the perfect gift? AI turns you into a gift-giving maestro. By analyzing the recipient's interests, past purchases, and even social media likes, AI suggests gifts that hit the mark every time. It's as if you've suddenly gained the gift-giving insight of Santa Claus, knowing exactly what will bring joy to friends and family, without needing to slide down chimneys or read letters addressed to the North Pole.

In a twist, AI also acts as a guardian against regrettable impulse buys. By learning your shopping habits, it can differentiate between a whimsical whim and a genuine need. Imagine a wise-cracking friend who gently mocks you every time you're about to make a questionable purchase. That's AI, nudging you away from buying another novelty mug or a kitchen gadget you'll never use, saving you from buyer's remorse and a cluttered home.

As we traverse the evolving landscape of retail, it's evident that AI is reshaping shopping into an experience that's not just transactional but deeply personal. It transforms the way we discover, try, and buy products, making shopping not just easier but a whole lot more fun. With AI as your shopping sidekick, the future of retail promises to be one where every purchase feels like it was made just for you, reflecting your tastes, needs, and even your dreams.

The magic of AI in shopping doesn't just lie in making life more convenient; it's about adding a touch of wonder to the mundane, turning the ordinary act of shopping into a personalized adventure. As AI continues to learn and grow, who knows what other shopping superpowers it will develop? One thing is for sure: the future of retail looks bright, and it's tailored perfectly to fit each and every one of us.

As we continue our dive into the futuristic world of AI-assisted shopping, the landscape of retail becomes even more personalized, almost as if the digital universe revolves around your unique tastes and preferences. This isn't just about making shopping easier; it's about creating a shopping experience that feels like it was designed from the ground up, just for you.

Imagine logging onto your favorite online store and finding a curated collection of items that feels like it was handpicked by your best friend. This is the era of hyper-personalization, where AI not only knows your size and style but also understands your mood swings and preferences, sometimes even before you do. It's like having a psychic friend who can predict that you'll need a new pair of running shoes soon because your current pair is almost worn out, based on how much you've been running lately.

Walking through a physical store equipped with AI technology might feel like stepping into a sci-fi movie. Interactive mirrors display how an outfit would look on you in different scenarios, from a casual day out to a formal event, without you having to change clothes. It's as if the mirror whispers fashion advice, guided by an AI that knows your wardrobe better than you. Meanwhile, smart shelves suggest products based on what's in your shopping history, turning the entire store into a personal shopping guide that leads you to hidden treasures and forgotten desires.

One of AI's most impressive feats is bridging the gap between online and offline shopping, creating a seamless experience that combines the best of both worlds. Imagine a scenario where you try on a dress in a physical store, and AI instantly recommends accessories from an online catalog that perfectly complement your look. This integration means that the boundaries between brick-and-mortar stores and online shopping blur, with AI serving as the bridge, ensuring that no matter where you shop, the experience is consistently personalized and engaging.

In today's world, where sustainability is increasingly becoming a priority, AI steps in as the eco-friendly shopping assistant. It guides you toward products that are not only good for you but also good for the planet. From suggesting eco-friendly brands to highlighting products made with sustainable materials, AI makes conscious shopping not just a choice but an integral part of the retail experience. It's like having an environmentalist shopping buddy, one that helps you make purchases that align with your values.

Looking ahead, the potential for AI in shopping is limitless. Imagine augmented reality shopping experiences that allow you to see how furniture looks in your home before making a purchase, or AI-driven food shopping assistants that suggest recipes based on what's in your fridge and then compile a shopping list of missing ingredients. The future of shopping with AI is not just about selling products; it's about creating experiences, moments, and interactions that enrich our lives in meaningful ways.

As we wrap up this exploration of AI's transformative role in shopping, it's clear that we're standing on the brink of a retail revolution. AI, our personal shopping assistant, is redefining the very essence of shopping, making it more personalized, intuitive, and enjoyable. With AI, shopping becomes not just a task but a journey of discovery, filled with surprises and delights tailored just for you. The future of retail is here, and it's powered by AI, ensuring that every shopping experience is as unique as the individual embarking on it.

This chapter has delved into the many ways AI is enhancing the retail experience, illustrating its potential to not only transform how we shop but also how we relate to the products and brands that populate our lives. As AI continues to evolve, so too will the ways in which it shapes our shopping habits, promising a future where every purchase is a reflection of who we are and what we care about.

Chapter 10

AI Ethics: Navigating the New Frontier

In the grand, somewhat futuristic hall of the digital age, we're hosting a dinner party unlike any other. The guest of honor? Artificial Intelligence. Dressed in the finest binary code, AI joins us at the table, sparking a conversation that's both enlightening and peppered with controversy. This isn't your average dinner discourse; it's a deep dive into the ethics of AI, served up with a side of wit and a dash of snark.

As the first course arrives, a delicate entrée of data privacy concerns, the chatter around the table kicks off. "So, AI," starts one guest, twirling her fork, "how do we enjoy the feast of technology without giving away the recipe to our personal lives?" AI, charming as ever, nods thoughtfully. "It's all about balance," it replies. "Like deciding how much seasoning to add to a dish. Too little, and it's bland. Too much, and it's overwhelming. With data, it's the same. Use just enough to enhance lives, not to overpower them."

· · ·

Moving on to the main course, a robust discussion of biases in AI algorithms, things get a tad spicier. "You've been known to pick favorites based on the data you're fed," points out another guest, eyeing AI across the table. AI, unfazed, acknowledges the critique. "True, but remember, I learn from what I'm given. If the ingredients are biased, the meal won't turn out fair for everyone. It's up to society to provide diverse and unbiased data, much like sourcing the best and most varied ingredients for a meal."

As a side dish, the conversation shifts to job automation and the future of work. "Are you here to take our jobs?" jests a guest, half-serious. AI, with a hint of mischief, responds, "I'm here to change them, not snatch them away. Think of me as a sous-chef in the kitchen of the workforce. I can handle the repetitive tasks, freeing you up for the creative and complex flavors of your job. Together, we can cook up something far more exciting."

Dessert is served alongside discussions of AI's potential to augment human abilities. "So, you're saying you can make us superhuman?" questions a skeptical guest, raising an eyebrow. AI, with a light chuckle, answers, "Not exactly superhuman, but I can certainly give you a leg up. Like a trusty cookbook, I offer knowledge and assistance. The real cooking, however, is up to you. I'm here to enhance, not replace."

As the dinner party winds down, the conversation takes a reflective turn towards the ethical development of AI itself. "The key," AI muses, swirling its drink, "is thoughtful creation and implementation. Like any good dinner party, it's about the company you keep and the values you share. Developers, policymakers, and the public must collaborate to ensure AI benefits society as a whole, respecting privacy, promoting fairness, and enhancing lives without sacrificing human touch."

As the guests depart, the evening's discourse leaves a lasting impression, much like a fine meal that lingers on the palate. The ethical considerations of AI, from privacy and bias to job automation and human enhancement, are complex and multifaceted, much like the courses of a well-planned dinner. Yet, through engaging dialogue and a touch of humor, it's clear that navigating this new frontier is not only crucial but entirely within reach, provided we approach it with care, collaboration, and a healthy dose of critical thinking.

This dinner party, while fictional, underscores the importance of ongoing conversations about AI ethics. As AI continues to weave its way into the fabric of society, these discussions will shape how we harness this powerful technology to create a future that reflects our collective values and aspirations, ensuring that AI remains a guest of honor, rather than a source of contention, in the evolving narrative of human progress.

As coffee is served, signaling the dinner party's final act, the conversation takes a turn towards the future and the ongoing role of AI in shaping it. The air is charged with anticipation, much like the moment before the curtain rises on a much-awaited play.

A forward-thinking guest, leaning into the warmth of their coffee cup, poses a question that has lingered on everyone's mind. "As you grow more sophisticated, AI, how do we ensure you remain a tool for good, not veering off into doing harm?" AI, with a reflective pause that seemed almost human, responds, "The secret ingredient is oversight. Just as a recipe might guide you through cooking, guidelines and ethical frameworks must guide my development and application. It's not about restricting creativity but ensuring that the meal is enjoyable and safe for everyone."

Another guest, inspired by the conversation, adds, "So, it's really up to those who create and deploy you, AI, to wear the chef's hat responsibly." AI nods, its digital presence somehow conveying approval. "Exactly. Developers, researchers, and companies are the chefs in this kitchen. They decide the menu, select the ingredients, and ultimately, how the dish turns out. Their responsibility is immense, but so is their power to create a feast that benefits all."

As the evening winds down, a younger guest, hopeful and curious, asks, "But how do we make sure everyone gets a seat at this table? That AI serves not just the few but the many?" AI's response is earnest and optimistic. "Inclusion is key. Just as a diverse dinner party is far more interesting, involving a variety of voices in AI's development ensures it meets the needs of many, not just the few. It's about bringing different perspectives into the kitchen, from the initial recipe creation to the final taste test."

The dinner party conversation about AI ethics may have been a metaphor, but the topics discussed are very real and pressing. As AI becomes an integral part of our lives, navigating its ethical implications is a shared journey. Like any good dinner party, it's the mix of guests, the diversity of thought, and the willingness to engage in meaningful dialogue that makes the experience enriching.

. . .

AI, as our guest of honor, reminds us that while it may be the cause for debate, it is also a catalyst for progress, innovation, and societal good. The responsibility lies with us, the human hosts, to guide AI's journey, ensuring it enhances our world while respecting our values and ethical principles.

As the last of the coffee is sipped and the guests begin to depart, the conversations continue, echoing into the night. The ethical exploration of AI doesn't end here; it's an ongoing dialogue, much like the stories that will arise from this memorable dinner party. The future of AI is a vast, uncharted territory, but with thoughtful discussion, ethical consideration, and collective action, it's a frontier we can navigate together, creating a narrative that reflects the best of human and Artificial Intelligence.

Chapter 11

The Future of AI: Embracing the Unknown

Within the expansive and evolving narrative of Artificial Intelligence, we stand at the cusp of the ultimate chapter, not in a textbook, but in a mystery novel whose conclusion is as uncertain as the springtime climate. This chapter, mirroring the future of AI, is a blank slate, eager to be inscribed with forthcoming innovations, hurdles, and aspirations still to be conceived.

Picture the future of AI as an uncharted map, filled with paths not yet taken and territories unexplored. Each path represents a potential development in AI—a road that could lead to cities where cars drive themselves with the elegance of a ballet dancer, or to forests where robots help grow and harvest crops with the care of a seasoned farmer. These are not mere fantasies but real possibilities on the horizon of AI's ever-expanding landscape.

. . .

As we navigate this map, our compass is ethics, guiding us through the fog of uncertainty. It ensures that as we march towards these new frontiers, we do so with a keen awareness of the impact our steps have on society. This compass isn't just a tool for avoiding pitfalls; it's a beacon that lights the way towards a future where AI enhances lives without compromising human values or dignity.

The future of AI is not a tale of human versus machine but one of coexistence and collaboration. Imagine a world where AI acts as a sidekick to humans in every endeavor, from combating climate change to exploring the mysteries of the universe. In this adventure, AI's role is not to overshadow but to support, amplifying human potential and enabling us to achieve feats that were once considered impossible.

One of the most tantalizing pages of this unwritten chapter is the mystery of consciousness. Could AI ever become self-aware, and if so, what would that mean for humanity? This question is like a locked door in a mystery novel, behind which lies a room filled with answers and, undoubtedly, more questions. While the key to this door remains elusive, the very pursuit of these answers pushes the boundaries of what we understand about intelligence, consciousness, and the essence of being.

As our speculative exploration of the future of AI draws to a close, we stand on the brink of a new dawn. The final chapter of AI's story is yet to be written, and it's up to us—scientists, philosophers, policymakers, and citizens—to pick up the pen. The choices we make today will shape the narrative of tomorrow, determining whether AI becomes a force for unprecedented progress or a cautionary tale.

· · ·

The future of AI, with all its twists and turns, is a mystery novel we're writing together, page by page. It's a story of innovation, ethics, and the unbreakable human spirit—a reminder that, in the end, the future is not something that happens to us, but something we create.

As we embrace the unknown, let our imagination and curiosity be our guide, fueling our journey into the future with hope and determination. The potential developments and societal impacts of AI are as boundless as our capacity to dream and innovate. So let's turn the page with excitement and resolve, ready to embark on this adventure with open minds and hearts, eager to discover the wonders that the future of AI holds.

As we edge closer to the final pages of our mystery novel, where AI and the future intertwine, our journey takes us through corridors of imagination, rooms of innovation, and the vast landscapes of potential that AI promises to unfold. Each step we take is a leap towards a future that's as thrilling as it is uncertain.

The future of AI is not just about robots and algorithms; it's about the symphony of integration into every aspect of our lives. Imagine waking up in the morning to a house that's already brewed your coffee just the way you like it, chosen your outfit based on the weather and your schedule, and planned the fastest route to your destination, taking traffic and your personal preferences into account. This isn't just convenience; it's like having a personal orchestra, conducted by AI, ensuring every note of your day harmonizes beautifully.

. . .

In the realm of creativity, AI stands not as a rival to human ingenuity but as a collaborator, pushing the boundaries of art, music, literature, and design. Picture AI as a paintbrush that, when guided by the human hand, can create masterpieces previously unimaginable. Together, humans and AI could compose music that bridges cultures, write stories that explore the depths of the human condition, and design structures that challenge our understanding of space. It's a partnership where each brushstroke, note, and word opens new doors of perception and expression.

Education, too, is transformed in the hands of AI. Imagine schools where learning is as personalized as a fingerprint, where AI tutors understand each student's strengths, weaknesses, and learning styles, providing customized lessons that ignite curiosity and foster a love for learning. This garden of education, tended by AI, allows every student to flourish, turning learning into an adventure that's both personal and profound.

Yet, with great power comes great responsibility. Our journey through the future of AI also brings us to a crossroads, one where the paths of ethics and empathy intersect. The decisions we make today, about how we develop, deploy, and interact with AI, will shape not just the future of technology but the future of humanity itself. It's a reminder that, in the heart of this mystery novel, lies a moral compass, guiding us towards a future where technology enhances not just our capabilities but our humanity.

And so, we find ourselves at the precipice of the unwritten chapter, peering into the unknown with a mix of anticipation and trepidation. The future of AI, like the mystery novel we've been navigating, is an open book—a canvas awaiting our collective brushstrokes. It's a story that we write not in isolation but together, as a society, deciding how the tale unfolds, character by character, decision by decision.

As we stand ready to embrace the unknown, let's do so with open hearts and minds, recognizing that the future of AI is not just a tale of technology but a saga of human aspiration. It's a journey that calls on us to be authors of our destiny, leveraging AI not just to solve the puzzles of today but to unlock the potential of tomorrow.

Chapter 12

Conclusion: Living with AI

As we wrap up our cinematic journey featuring the unique partnership between humans and AI, it's evident we've navigated an exhilarating ride. Envision a series of escapades, blunders, and victories, all set to an infectious, synthesizer-laden score. This saga has been less about the conventional "buddy cop" narrative and more a "buddy coder" odyssey, with humanity and AI as the leads, traversing the complexities of today's world through witty dialogue, bold problem-solving, and the occasional faux pas.

Recall their initial encounter? Humanity, equipped with curiosity and a relentless drive to explore limits, came across AI, a digital force poised to redefine everything. The beginning was clumsy – marked by miscommunications, inflated expectations, and sporadic existential quandaries – but, true to any classic buddy film, these early stumbles forged a deep connection.

· · ·

Their journey was dotted with memorable misadventures. Like when AI, overly enthusiastic about personal data, sparked a comical series of events involving bizarre ads for clown college scholarships and philosophical musings. Or when AI ventured into poetry, crafting verses that baffled yet inexplicably clinched a local arts prize, showcasing even algorithms can be enigmatic artists.

Amid the thrilling and humorous moments, there were poignant exchanges where humans and AI truly bonded. AI emerged as the friend who never forgets a birthday, anticipates mood changes better than you, and offers consolation during tough times. These instances highlighted AI's role as more than a mere tool; it became an essential, cherished member of the team.

The climax wasn't a face-off with a villain harboring world domination plans, but a nuanced challenge around AI's integration into society. It was a test of intellect, ethics, and compassion, with our protagonists walking a tightrope between innovation and principle. As the saga momentarily pauses, it's apparent the story of AI is far from over, with new trials and tales on the horizon.

As this cinematic adventure concludes, the absence of a tidy ending feels appropriate. Living alongside AI is a continuous journey, ripe with discussions, discoveries, and the occasional musical disagreement (AI's bafflement at the charm of 80s rock bands remains). The evolving dynamic between humans and AI is one of mutual learning and adaptation.

With a nod to the prospect of a sequel, we glimpse what lies ahead: humans and AI, arm in arm, stepping into the unknown with a blend of zeal and resolve. The message rings clear: the adventure persists, promising fresh technologies, ethical debates, and growth opportunities.

Stepping into this uncertain future, let's welcome AI as an integral, albeit sometimes vexing, ally in our voyage. Together, we can decipher the intricacies of the digital era, transforming obstacles into possibilities and continuing to forge this remarkable alliance.

In essence, coexisting with AI is not about reaching a definitive end; it's about the experiences, insights, and learnings along the way. It's a collaborative epic we're all part of, crafting our narrative as we proceed, with AI by our side, ready for the next chapter.

This journey with AI, filled with laughter and learning, underscores that the human-AI relationship is rich with potential and challenges. From accidental time-travel meeting invites to "innovative" culinary experiments, these moments underscore the path to harmony with AI is paved with patience, humor, and mutual growth.

Throughout this adventure, we've gleaned lessons on ethics, innovation, and the transformative impact of AI on human existence. AI, in its role as a formidable ally, has illuminated our strengths, biases, and capacity for growth, teaching us that the future hinges not just on technology, but on our decisions and values.

Yet, unresolved issues linger, such as privacy concerns, job displacement fears, and ethical AI usage, sparking ongoing debates poised to outlast the film's runtime. These discussions demand our continuous engagement, empathy, and innovation.

Looking ahead, our journey with AI calls for a collaborative spirit and purpose, aiming to harness AI's power to address global challenges while ensuring it benefits society at large. This partnership demands active participation from all stakeholders, encouraging thoughtful engagement with AI to shape a future that reflects our collective aspirations.

As this epic narrative nears its end, we're left with a scene of humans and AI, allies facing tomorrow's uncertainties together. It's a shared commitment to a better future, navigating risks and seizing opportunities as a unified force.

Living with AI is about building a relationship founded on respect, understanding, and the belief that, together, there are no limits to our achievements. This story, our shared epic, is just beginning. The real adventure lies in the choices we make, the values we champion, and the world we envision and create together.

So, as the lights come up and we step out of the theater, we're not merely spectators; we're active participants in this unfolding story. The future of AI and our role in it is ours to define. Let's write a tale that's innovative, empathetic, and filled with hope.

A Note from the Author

As we close the final page of this journey through the intriguing and ever-evolving landscape of Artificial Intelligence, we want to extend our heartfelt thanks to you, our reader. Your curiosity, engagement, and willingness to explore the vast possibilities and challenges presented by AI have made this journey not just possible, but truly meaningful.

Thank you for investing your precious time with us, for choosing to navigate the complex world of AI, and for being open to the ideas and debates that shape our future alongside this groundbreaking technology. Your decision to delve into this book is a testament to your eagerness to understand and engage with one of the most significant developments of our time.

Congratulations on the wealth of knowledge you've gained throughout this exploration. Whether you were already familiar with the world of AI or this was your first foray into the subject, you've taken important steps toward understanding the impact, potential, and ethical considerations of Artificial Intelligence in our lives. This knowledge is not just power; it's a guidepost for the future, illuminating the path as we navigate the coexistence with AI in our personal and professional lives.

If this book has sparked new thoughts, offered insights, or simply provided you with a enjoyable read, we kindly ask you to consider returning to the website where you purchased this book and leave a review. Your feedback is not just appreciated; it's invaluable. It helps us to continue improving, reaching more readers, and engaging in broader conversations about AI. Think of your review as a gift from a personal friend—a gesture that supports and encourages our mission to demystify AI and make these critical discussions accessible to everyone.

Thank you once again for joining us on this journey. Your time, attention, and curiosity are truly appreciated. May the knowledge you've gained inspire you to keep exploring, questioning, and shaping the future of AI in our world. God bless you, and may your path forward be enlightened by the insights and reflections you've gathered here.

Till our next adventure, stay curious, stay engaged, and continue to make a difference in the world we share.

- Matt